Learn the Maltese Language: Maltese grammar easily explained
by Alain de Raymond

© Alain de Raymond, 2016
All rights reserved

To everyone who supported me while writing this book – especially my parents.

Table of Contents

Introduction: learning Maltese 7
Chapter 1: the alphabet 9
Chapter 2: to be and the personal pronouns 11
Chapter 3: the imperative 12
Chapter 4: the present tense 13
Chapter 5: the infinitive 15
Chapter 6: to have 17
Chapter 7: the negative 18
Chapter 8: the past tense 19
Chapter 9: the future tense 22
Chapter 10: the present (perfect) and past continuous 24
Chapter 11: present participle 26
Chapter 12: past perfect 27
Chapter 13: the article 28
Chapter 14: nouns 29
Chapter 15: adjectives 30
Chapter 16: comparative and superlative 32
Chapter 17: demonstrative pronouns 33
Chapter 18: prepositions 34
Chapter 19: attached pronouns 36
Chapter 20: possessive 39
Chapter 21: my name is, exception 40
Chapter 22: interrogative pronouns 41
Chapter 23: adverbs 42
Chapter 24: numbers 43
Chapter 25: time 47
Bonus 1: Maltese cities and their meaning 48

Bonus 2: study further on the internet.................................51
The final word – About the author..53

Introduction: learning Maltese

Hi, my name is Alain from Belgium. I learnt Maltese for 2.5 years when I was living in Malta. Truth is: you don't need that much time to understand Maltese grammar at a basic level.

The Maltese language may seem very **complicated**. There aren't many online resources, there are very few Maltese language schools, and the grammar sometimes doesn't make any sense. Especially the Arabic parts can be very challenging for those who don't know Arabic.

And that's why I wrote this book to learn Maltese. Before, I already made a free[1] and an extended[2] Maltese online course. The purpose is to have readers think 'If I had known this book existed… I wouldn't have had so much trouble.'

Grammar is important. However, it is even more important to **speak, write, read** and **listen** to Maltese! Apply what you learn in this book in your everyday conversations, in your letters, listening while waiting for the bus… Only exercise makes masters!

The book covers the Maltese grammar without getting into too much detail. It includes many examples and practical help in an easy way.

---

[1] https://wp.me/P9L3un-l

[2] https://bit.ly/3WeVX3G

It starts with **pronunciation**, continues with the **tenses** of the verb, **nouns**, **pronouns**, and **adjectives** as well as **numbers** and **time**. In the bonus section, you will find **Maltese towns** and their meaning and a list of mainly **free resources** to study more Maltese.

Happy learning,

Alain

Chapter 1: the alphabet

Let's start with how to pronounce Maltese with the alphabet. It is very similar to the English alphabet. The **bold letters** have a different or special pronunciation.

Aa Bb **Ċċ** Dd Ee Ff **Ġġ** Gg **Għgħ Hh Ħħ Ii Ieie** Jj Kk Ll Mm Nn Oo Pp **Qq** Rr Ss Tt **Uu** Vv Ww **Xx Żż** Zz

- Ċċ: like **ch**eck
- Ġġ: like **G**eorge
- Gg: like **g**reat
- Għgħ: unpronounced, in Maltese "għajn"
- Hh: unpronounced, in Maltese "akka", unless it is at the end of a word, then it is pronounced like ħ
- Ħħ: like **h**ard, but a little harder
- Ii: like f**ea**r
- Ieie: longer than i
- Jj: like **y**ounger
- Qq: like **(**)archer, the sound before archer but a little harder
- Uu: like y**ou**
- Xx: like **sh**ort
- Żż: like **z**oo
- Zz: like **ts**unami

The **għ** does influence the pronunciation of other letters. If after an 'i', as in 'ngħid' (I tell), the għi is pronounced like the i in pr**i**de. If it is written at the end of a word, it takes the 'ħ' sound.

9

However, the għ is unpronounced when it is hidden. In that case, the għ is written like ' as in nista' (I can).

Note that there is no c in the Maltese alphabet, only ċ. The 'u' changes into a 'w' if the word before ends with a vowel. **Two vowels never follow each other** directly in a word. Between words, they are avoided but it can still happen.

Watch out when you're looking for a word in the **dictionary**. For example, when you're looking for a word starting with għ, don't look for it at the letter g.

Links on the internet:

Find more about the Maltese alphabet on Wikipedia:
https://en.wikipedia.org/wiki/Maltese_alphabet

Hear the alphabet on:
https://youtu.be/NteVAgibWes

Chapter 2: to be and the personal pronouns

The personal pronouns are the following:

I = jien / jiena	We = aħna
You = int / inti	You = intom
He = hu / huwa	They = huma
She = hi / hija	

In the singular, both options can be used and mean the same. A trick to remember the conjugation: the 1st, 2nd and 3rd person are similar, for example int and intom. Mind that if 'you' is just one person, to use int or inti. But if 'you' is more than one person, use intom. 'It' doesn't exist in Maltese, and there is no politeness form.

The pronoun is only used to **stress the subject** of the verb. For example if you want to stress that it is you who's working, and not the others, you say: 'Jiena naħdem.' In other cases, you say: 'Naħdem'.

The verb **'to be' doesn't exist** in the present tense. Instead, a pronoun is used without any verb. Words like 'hemm' (= there) and 'hawn' (= here) can also replace the use of 'to be'. For example: Hemm Jean. (= Jean is there).

Chapter 3: the imperative

Maltese verbs have both a **singular and a plural** imperative. It depends if you direct it at one or at more than one person or animal. Usually, the plural ends with –u, as in:

- Aħdem – aħdmu (= work!)
- Għid – għidu (= tell!)

If there are two or more vowels, as in a**ħde**m, the 'u' will normally eat the last vowel. Some verbs' imperative end with –a and –aw.

- Ara – araw (= look!)
- Aqra – aqraw (= read!)

Others end with an accent. This accent is the hidden letter għ, which appears in the plural. The 'a' is eaten here by the 'u' in the plural.

- Ista'- istgħu (= be able to!)
- Erġa' – erġgħu (= repeat!)

Chapter 4: the present tense

The present tense uses the imperative (see previous chapter) as a basis. It uses the singular imperative for the singular, and the plural imperative for the plural. In the singular, it puts **N-T-J-T** in front of the imperative, and in the plural **N-T-J**. In Maltese, there is no female plural. Some examples we've already seen the imperative of:

Naħdem (I work)	**N**aħdmu (we work)
Taħdem (you work)	**T**aħdmu (you work)
Jaħdem (he works)	**J**aħdmu (they work)
Taħdem (she works)	

Nara (I look)	Naraw (we look)
Tara (you look)	Taraw (you look)
Jara (he looks)	Jaraw (they look)
Tara (she looks)	

Nista' (I can)	Nistgħu (we can)
Tista' (you can)	Tistgħu (you can)
Jista' (he can)	Jistgħu (they can)
Tista' (she can)	

Note that the 'you' in the singular and the 'she' have the same conjugation.

The present tense is often presented in complex ways. There are a number of exceptions, such as to be, but most verbs use the conjugation above. You **only** need to **remember the imperative** and the **endings** to conjugate most verbs.

Other exceptions are when the imperative starts with two consonants, which make it different to pronounce. An 'i' is added to the conjugations, but not in the imperative:

- Imperative: tkellem / tkellmu (= speak!)

Nitkellem (I speak)	Nitkellmu (we speak)
Titkellem (you speak)	Titkellmu (you speak)
Jitkellem (he speaks)	Jitkellmu (they speak)
Titkellem (she speaks)	

In certain cases, an **'i' is added** if the word before ends with a consonant. It also often happens that the 'j' just before a consonant changes into an 'i' after a consonant, as in jmur/imur.

immur / mmur (I go)	immorru / mmorru (we go)
tmur (you go)	
jmur / imur (he goes)	tmorru (you go)
tmur (she goes)	jmorru / imorru (they go)

There are a number of other exceptions. If in doubt, you might find all the conjugations back on this free online dictionary: www.maltesedictionary.org.mt

A last remark: if you use two verbs, for example 'I can work', you conjugate twice: Nista' naħdem. The second verb is not an infinitive.

Chapter 5: the infinitive

The Maltese language doesn't have an infinitive. To find a verb in the dictionary, it uses the 'mamma', or verb stem. It's the third person male in the past (see chapter 8), for example ħadem for 'he worked'.

However, it is crucial to know that this verb stem is made up of a few **key consonants**, usually 3. For 'to work', it's ħ, d and m. These consonants will be used in all conjugations of the verb 'to work', like naħdem and ħadem.

It's important to understand that in Maltese, **consonants** are much **more important** than vowels. That is why the key consonants of many verbs are used to make nouns and adjectives. For example:

- Xemx (sun)
- Xmux (suns)
- Xemxi (sunny)
- Xemxata (sunstroke)
- Nxemmex (I sunbathe)
- Xemmixtx (I didn't sunbathe)

Note that the order of the consonants may change, and that not all consonants are as important as the other ones. The root consonants are the most important ones, in this case **x-m-x**.

Thanks to this, you will understand many Maltese words. For this example, every time you see or hear 'x-m-x' very close to one another, you can suspect it has something to do with the sun, even though you might not know the exact word or conjugation. However, always **beware**: timxix means 'don't walk!' and has no relation to anything sunny.

Tip: if you type in a word in this online dictionary: www.maltesedictionary.org.mt, you will find many related entries. Try xemx. You will also find the 'root', which are the key consonants.

Chapter 6: to have

The verb to have in Maltese is **irregular** and frequently used. It also has **endings** that will be used in pronouns (-i/ni, -ek/ok, -u, -ha, -na, -kom, -hom). The conjugation changes in the ending, unlike other verbs:

Għandi (= I have)	Għandna (= we have)
Għandek (= you have)	Għandkom (= you have)
Għandu (= he has)	Għandhom (= they have)
Għandha (= she has)	

To have is also used for '**to have to, to must**'. In that case, the conjugated verb is added to the conjugation of to have: 'Għandi naħdem', I have to work.

Note that the conjugation of the verb to have can also be used as a noun. It is translated as 'what I/you/… owns', and generally refers to one's home. 'Għandi' would be 'my home'.

Chapter 7: the negative

In Maltese, the negative is normally used with a verb by putting '**ma**' in front of the verb and attaching '**x**' to the verb, as in:

- Naħdmu (we work) – ma naħdmux (we don't work).

When a conjugation ends with –a, the a turns into ie, as in għandha (she has), ma għandhiex (se doesn't have). An e before a consonant sometimes become i, as in naħdem (I work), ma naħdimx (I don't work).

The **–x disappears** if the verb uses a negative pronoun like qatt (never) and xejn (nothing). For example qatt ma naħdem (I never work).

When the verb starts with a vowel, h or j, the ma becomes m' or is added to the verb. For example hu (it/he is) becomes mhux (it/he is not). The ma is **dropped** for the **negative imperative**, which is in the second person. For example: taħdimx / taħdmux (don't work!).

See also the exception in the first person singular of to be, the ie of **jiena** is shortened to i:

M'iniex (I am not)	M'aħniex
M'intix (you are not)	M'intomx
Mhux (he/it is not)	M'humiex
Mhix (she is not)	

Don't confuse the ma from the negative with the ma' from the prepositions (see chapter 18). The preposition has a ' at the end.

Chapter 8: the past tense

The past tense is the most difficult Maltese tense to learn. Let's start with short verbs. The endings (-t, -t, -, -et, -na, -tu, -u) are in **bold**:

Għed**t** (I said)	Għed**na** (we said)
Għed**t** (you said)	Għed**tu** (you said)
Qal (he said)	Qal**u** (they said)
Qal**et** (she said)	

Verbs in the past have two roots. There is one for the 1st and 2nd person (għed in this case) and there is the verb stem (qal in this case) for the 3rd person. You will find the verb stem in the dictionary.

Note that I and you have the same conjugation in the singular. Let's see a variation:

Rajt (I saw)	Rajna (we saw)
Rajt (you saw)	Rajtu (you saw)
Ra (he saw)	Raw (they saw)
Rat (she saw)	

If the root of the 3rd person ends with a vowel, it eats the e in the 3rd person female: it's rat instead of raet. Note as well that the raw takes the w of the present tense (jaraw).

Longer verbs have also two roots in the past. However, in the 3rd person in the female and plural, the **last vowel is eaten**.

Ħdimt (I worked)	Ħdimna (we worked)
Ħdimt (you worked)	Ħdimtu (you worked)
Ħadem (he worked)	Ħadmu (they worked)
Ħadmet (she worked)	

Note that the **root consonants** are the same as for the present (naħdem) as for the past (ħdimt): ħ, d and m. There are exceptions. For example to say, which is għid in the present. The first root takes the għ and d over in għedt, but not in qal.

To learn the past, one must **only learn** the **two roots**, apply the **endings** and let the last vowel in the third person female and plural be eaten in case there's more than one vowel.

A trick to help you find the present or past: most verbs' single imperative's first two letters change places to become the verb stem (3rd single past):

- **Aħ**dem (work!) becomes **ħa**dem (he worked)
- **Aq**ra (read!) becomes **qa**ra (he read)
- **Is**ta' (be able to!) becomes **se**ta (he was able to)

To be is not an exception. It has a conjugation, unlike the present tense.

Kont	Konna
Kont	Kontu
Kien	Kienu
Kienet	

To have is different though. It continues to use the endings of the present, but with 'kell' as a root.

Kelli (I had)	Kellna (we had)
Kellek (you had)	Kellkom (you had)
Kellu (he had)	Kellhom (they had)
Kellha (she had)	

In combination with another verb, it means 'had to', as in 'Kelli naħdem.' I had to work. Note that the other verb is in the present tense.

To use 'not yet', the past is used in combination with the negative and għadni, għadek, għadu, għadha, għadna, għadkom, għadhom. It is translated as 'to have', but mind the 'n' is missing, e.g. għadek vs għandek. An example for not yet: 'għadni ma ħadimx', I haven't worked yet.

Chapter 9: the future tense

The future tense is very easy. Just use **se** in front of the conjugation of the present tense, and you have it. For example:

Se naħdem (I will work)	Se naħdmu (we will work)
Se taħdem (you will work)	Se taħdmu (you will work)
Se jaħdem (he will work)	Se jaħdmu (they will work)
Se taħdem (she will work)	

Se comes from the verb **sejjer**. It can be shortened as 'sa' as well, and can be kept in full: sejjer (male), **sejra** (female), **sejrin** (plural).

If the person speaking is a man, he will say sejjer naħdem. A woman would say sejra naħdem. Together, they would say sejrin naħdmu.

To be is conjugated in the future as follows:

Nkun (I will be)	Nkunu (we will be)
Tkun (you will be)	Tkunu (you will be)
Jkun (he will be)	Jkunu (they will be)
Tkun (she will be)	

To have is another exception, using the endings of the present and the past with ikoll as root:

ikolli (I will have)	ikollna (we will have)
ikollok (you will have)	ikollkom (you will have)
ikollu (he will have)	ikollhom (they will have)
ikollha (she will have)	

The conjugation of to have in combination with another verb in the present means **I'll have to, I must**, as in:

- Ikolli naħdem (I should work)

Chapter 10: the present (perfect) and past continuous

The Maltese **present continuous** is relatively easy. Just put an 'qed' in front of the conjugated verb in the present, and you have it.

Qed naħdem (I am working)	Qed naħdmu (we are working)
Qed taħdem (you are working)	Qed taħdmu (you are working)
Qed jaħdem (he is working)	Qed jaħdmu (they are working)
Qed taħdem (she is working)	

However, similarly to the future tense (se becomes sejjer), qed can become **qiegħed** (male), **qiegħda** (female) and **qegħdin** (plural). This is for your passive knowledge, as Maltese speakers use it while you can always use qed.

So a man would say qiegħed naħdem (I am working), a woman qiegħda naħdem (I am working) and together it would be qegħdin naħdmu (we are working).

When there is no verb joined to qed or one of the other forms, it means the verb to be should be added and it is translated as 'staying at, being present'. For example 'qed fil-kamra' would mean 'I am currently in the room.'

To make the **past continuous**, just put the past of to be in front of the present continuous, as in:

- Kont qed naħdem (I was working)

To make the **present perfect** continuous, Maltese uses il + the endings of to have (ili, ilek, ilu, ilha, ilna, ilkom and ilhom) plus the present tense of the verb.

- Ili naħdem sentejn (I have been working for two years)

Chapter 11: present participle

The Maltese present participle is made by **m** + the verb's **imperative**. The last vowel changes into u and sometimes i. For example with the verb agħmel – agħmlu (to make), the present participle is:

- Magħmul, magħmula, magħmulin (= made)

The present participle behaves like an adjective in Maltese (see chapter 15) and so it depends on the noun that it stands with whether it's magħmul (male), magħmula (female) or magħmulin (plural).

Chapter 12: past perfect

The past perfect in Maltese is a combination of the past of **to be** plus the past of the other tense. For example:

- Kien ħadem (= he had worked)

Chapter 13: the article

Maltese has **no indefinite article** ('a', although it can be expressed, see chapter 24) but it does have a definite article ('the'), which is used more often than the English 'the'. It usually is 'il-', as in:

- il-kelma (the word)
- il-ħin (the time)

When the noun starts with **ċ, d, n, r, s, t, x, z,** or **ż**, the L is replaced by the first letter of the noun, for example:

- is-sett (set)
- id-dar (house, home)

Tip: most of these letters are the last consonants of the alphabet. If the word before end with a vowel, or the noun starts with one, the **'i' is dropped**, as in:

- Inti l-mara? vs Int il-mara? (mara = woman, wife)
- L-arja (air)

When nouns start with certain combinations of letters (rg, md, st, sk) the i moves to the noun, as in:

- L-iskola (school)
- L-Imdina (city in Malta)

Note that the i is also dropped at the beginning of certain verbs (see chapter 4). One last remark: names of persons (e.g. Mark, Sarah) never take the article.

Chapter 14: nouns

Maltese nouns are **either male or female**. Most nouns ending with –a are female, like kelma.

General nouns like 'water' or 'people' are more frequently used in Maltese than in English. Especially food items have many general nouns. The general noun takes the male form, one item takes the female form (+a) and the plural is rarely used, for example for exact numbers.

- Ħut (fish)
- Ħuta (one fish)
- Ħutiet (fishes)

The plural of nouns (and adjectives) have the following endings: **-i, -in, -n, -t, -at, -iet, -ijiet, -an, -ien**. A number of nouns have a dual plural. It's a plural just to indicate two items. Most are related to time, body and weight. For example:

- Jum (day), jumejn (two days), jiem (days)

The dual plurals end with –ejn or –ajn.

Chapter 15: adjectives

Maltese **adjectives follow the noun** it stands with, unlike in English. Adjectives have a male, female and plural form:

- Ir-raġel kbir (the big man)
- Id-dar kbira (the big house)
- Id-djar kbar (the big houses)

The female form is usually the male + a. If the male form ends with –i, it becomes -ja. Note that the **article can be added** in front of the adjectives derived from Arabic, if it is just after the noun:

- Ir-raġel il-kbir (the big man)
- Id-dar il-kbira (the big house)
- Id-djar il-kbar (the big houses)

It is not necessary, but remember it can happen. Adjectives coming from Italian normally **end with –i** and don't change:

- Ir-raġel importanti (the important man)
- Id-dar importanti (the important house)
- Id-djar importanti (the important houses)

Nationalities take –a for the female and –i for the plural:

- Taljan, Taljana, Taljani (Italian)

But Maltese are an exception:

- Malti, Maltija, Maltin (Maltese)

Note that the present participle (see chapter 11) behaves just like adjectives, for example:

- Ir-raġel magħruf (from għaraf, to recognise, to be known): the famous man
- Il-mara magħrufa: the famous woman
- Id-djar magħrufin: the famous houses

Chapter 16: comparative and superlative

Adjectives with a vowel or coming from non-Semitic languages use **aktar** (more) or **iżjed** (more) in front of the adjective, as in:

- Aktar importanti (more important)

Semitic adjectives have an own comparative, but are more and more used with aktar as well.

- Kbar (big) - ikbar (bigger) – aktar kbar (bigger)

The first comparative usually puts an **i or an e in front of the adjective**. If the adjective has more than one syllable, the two first letters (consonant and a vowel) switch positions. The vowel turns into an i or an e.

- **Sa**biħ (nice, beautiful) – **is**baħ (nicer, more beautiful)

The **superlative** is the comparative with an article in front:

- L-ikbar (the biggest)
- L-isbaħ (the most beautiful)
- L-aktar importanti (the most important)

Chapter 17: demonstrative pronouns

Maltese demonstrative pronouns have the same structure as in English. However, they adapt to the **gender**.

Dan raġel (this is a man) Dak raġel (that is a man)	Din mara (this is a woman) Dik mara (that is a woman)
Dawn djar (these are houses) Dawk djar (those are houses)	

If the verb to be is not used, an **article** needs to be placed in front of the noun.

Dan ir-raġel (this man) Dak ir-raġel (that man)	Din il-mara (this woman) Dik il-mara (that woman)
Dawn id-djar (these houses) Dawk id-djar (those houses)	

Dan, din and dawn **can be joined** to the article: e.g. dar-raġel.

Chapter 18: prepositions

In Maltese, prepositions are often used. The prepositions are **joined to the article** (il-) if there is one. They are:

	Translation	With article	Without article
Bi	With (objects & animals)	Bil-	B'
Fi	in	Fil-	F'
Ġo	In, inside	Ġol-	Ġo
Bħal	Like	Bħall-	Bħal
Għal	For	Għall-	Għal
Lil	To	Lill-	Lil
Sa	Until, as far as	Sal-	S'
Ta'	of	Tal-	Ta'
Ma'	With (persons)	Mal-	Ma'
minn	from	Mill-	minn

Note that sa, bi an fi change into **s'**, **b'** and **f'** in front of nouns without an article. Prepositions take over the changes of the article (see chapter 13), for example:

- Fl-iskola (in the school)
- Tad-dar (of the house)

Note that fi is more often used than ġo. Ġo can only be used for objects.

Some verbs take specific prepositions. For example to think about:

- Naħseb fik (I think about you, see next chapter)

Chapter 19: attached pronouns

Attached pronouns can be added to prepositions, nouns and verbs to specify whom it is addressing. The conjugations are the endings of the verb 'to have' (see chapter 6):

-ni / -i / -ja	-na
-ek / -ok / -k	-kom
-u / -h	-hom
-ha	

Note that the underlined –ja / -k / -h are used for **words ending with vowels**. –i is only used for verbs.

Added to the prepositions of the previous chapter, the attached pronouns add whom is concerned, for example with (second row of the table) me (second column of the table) or from him.

	me	you	him	her
With	Bija	bik	bih	biha
In	fija	fik	fih	fiha
Like	bħali	bħalek	bħalu	bħalha
For	għali	għalek	għalu	għalha
To	lili	lilek	lilu	lilha
Of	tiegħi	tiegħek	tiegħu	tagħha
With	miegħi	miegħek	miegħu	magħha

	us	**you**	**them**
With	bina	bikom	bihom
In	fina	fikom	fihom
Like	bħalna	bħalkom	bħalhom
For	għalna	għalkom	għalhom
To	lilna	lilkom	lilhom
Of	tagħna	tagħkom	tagħhom
With	magħna	magħkom	magħhom

Note that in the two last rows, the ie changes into an a from the 3rd female person on.

Attached pronouns can be **added to nouns** to determine who possesses the noun. This can happen with relatives, body parts and a number of exceptions.

- E.g. ommi (my mother), rasek (your head), daru (his house)

Other nouns use mine (of me), yours (of you)… for example:

- is-sett tagħna (our set).

With **verbs**, just add the attached pronoun:
- Jarani (he sees me)
- Jarak (he sees you)
- Jarah (he sees him)
- Jaraha (he sees her)
- Jarana (he sees us)
- Jarakom (he sees you)
- Jarahom (he sees them)

However, if the attached pronoun can be translated as 'to/for' a person/something (= the indirect object), the verb will use the shortened version of lil-. See for example:
- Jgħid**li** (he tells 'to' me)
- Jgħid**lek** (he tells you)
- Jgħid**lu** (he tells him)
- Jgħid**lha** (he tells her)
- Jgħid**lna** (he tells us)
- Jgħid**lkom** (he tells you)
- Jgħid**lhom** (he tells them)

However, it can become complicated when translating 'he tells it to them'. It will be translated as follows:
- Jgħid**hulhom**

'It' can be in the male (**hu**), in the female (**hie/ha**) and in the plural (**hom**) and is written before the indirect object (l-), as in the example jgħid<u>hu</u>lhom.

Chapter 20: possessive

We've seen two ways to express the possessive. First one is simply by using the **preposition** ta':

- Id-dar tar-raġel (the house of the man)

Another way is the **possessive pronoun**, either loose or attached (see the previous chapter):

- Daru (his house) and settu (his set)
- Dar tiegħu (his house) and sett tiegħu (his set)

Chapter 21: my name is, exception

To express one's name, a noun behaves like a verb:

Jisimni (my name is)	Jisimna (our name is)
Jismek (your name is)	Jisimkom (your name is)
Jismu (his name is)	Jisimhom (their name is)
Jisimgha (her name is)	

It is composed as follows **j + isem + attached pronoun (+ present tense of to be)**.

Isem is the noun (<u>name</u>). J- is the conjugation (<u>the</u> name <u>is</u>). Because isem is male it isn't t-. The attached pronoun (-ni) determines whose name it is (<u>my</u> name is) and the verb to be is not shown (my name <u>is</u> (see chapter 2)).

Chapter 22: interrogative pronouns

Maltese has interrogative pronouns just like English. They stand in front of the sentences just before the verb:

- Xi /x' (what)
- Fejn (where)
- Min (who)
- Meta (when)
- Liema (which)
- Għaliex (why)
- Għalfejn (for what reason)

Don't confuse **minn** (from, see chapter 18) and **min** (who). Note that x' lets the personal pronouns hu, hi and huma take an in-. It becomes x'inhu (what is it?) x'inhi (what is it?) and x'inhuma (what are they?).

Xi also means some, as in **xi djar** (some houses), **xi ħadd** (someone) and **xi ħaġa** (something). If it stands on its own, it is written '**xiex**' as in:

- Min jagħmel xiex? (who does what?)

Chapter 23: adverbs

Adverbs in Maltese have, like in English, no male, female or plural form. Some examples are:

- Hemm (there)
- Wisq (too much)
- Issa (now)

Many adverbs that are translated with –ly at the end in English, use the ending **–ment**. Some use bil- at the beginning.

- Normalment (normally)
- Bilkemm (hardly)

Chapter 24: numbers

In Malta, Maltese numbers are rarely used. Their main use is to **indicate the time** (see the next chapter). For prices, Maltese people usually use English. So up to twelve one has to actively know. However, a passive knowledge is always good. Here are the first 20 numbers:

0	żero	10	għaxra
1	wieħed/ waħda	11	ħdax
2	tnejn	12	tnax
3	tlieta	13	tlettax
4	erbgħa	14	erbatax
5	ħamsa	15	ħmistax
6	sitta	16	sittax
7	sebgħa	17	sbatax
8	tmienja	18	tmintax
9	disgħa	19	dsatax
		20	għoxrin

Note that number one adapts to the gender can have **two meanings**. It depends on the position of the number.

- Mara waħda = one woman
- Waħda mara = a woman (could be seen as an indefinite article)

Number 11 to 19 end with –ax and use an **article attached** to the number with nouns. The article does not adapt to the noun, for example it is not –id in:

- Ħdax-il djar (11 houses)

Don't confuse the number 2 to 4 to the **days of the week**, which are written with article and with capital in Maltese. In many Arab countries, Sunday is the first day of the week so that's why Monday is based on the number 2.

- It-Tnjen (Monday)
- It-Tlieta (Tuesday)
- L-Erbgħa (Wednesday)
- Il-Ħamis (Thursday)
- Il-Ġimgħa (Friday)
- Is-Sibt (Saturday)
- Il-Ħadd (Sunday)

From **2 to 10, the number adapts** if it's used with a noun. The ordinal numbers are also added in the last column. For example 'first' is 'l-ewwel'. After 10, it is simply the article plus the number, for example il-ħdax (the eleventh).

	2+ syllable	**1-syllable**	l-ewwel
tnejn	żewġ	żewġt	It-tieni
tlieta	tliet	tlett	It-tielet
erbgħa	erba'	erbat	Ir-raba'
ħamsa	ħames	ħamest	Il-ħames
sitta	sitt	sitt	Is-sitt
sebgħa	seba'	sebat	Is-seba'
tmienja	tmien	tmint	It-tmien
disgħa	disa'	disat	Id-disa'
għaxra	għaxar	għaxart	l-għaxar

The second column shows the number for nouns with **more than one syllable**, like Taljani: ħames Taljani (5 Italians). The third column is for nouns of **one syllable**, like djar: sitt djar (6 houses).

From **20 on, the numbers are combined** with 1-9:

- Wieħed u għoxrin (21)
- Tnejn u għoxrin (22)
- Tlieta u għoxrin (23)

Note that 'u' means 'and', and that the **1-9 come in front** of the 20, not like in English: twenty-one.

So the other multiplications of 10 are:
- Tletin (30)
- Erbgħin (40)
- Ħamsin (50)
- Sittin (60)
- Sebgħin (70)
- Tmenin (80)
- Disgħin (90)

100 is **mija** (mitt with nouns). Fil-mija is per cent (which means per 100 in Latin's per centum). 1000 is **elf** and a million is **miljun**.

You can find more explanations and examples on numbers on: https://www.youtube.com/watch?v=IMplo6MZ7_I.

Chapter 25: time

Asking for the time is '**x'ħin hu?**' in Maltese. When replying, use the numbers (1-11) with an article. Here is the vocabulary:

siegħa	One o'clock (also 'hour')
Nofsinhar / nofs in-nhar	Midday (no article)
Nofsilejl / nofs il-lejl	Midnight (no article)
kwart	quarter
nofs	half
u	Past (also 'and')
nieqes	to

Examples:
- 13:30 is is-siegħa u nofs,
- 14:45 is it-tlieta nieqes kwart
- 16:00 is l-erbgħa

Note that '**at**' is translated with **fi**:
- At 16:00 is fl-erbgħa
- At 12:00 is f'nofsinhar

Bonus 1: Maltese cities and their meaning

Here's a list of Maltese cities that have a meaning in the Maltese language.

Il-Belt Valletta: il-belt means the city. Valletta, Malta's capital, is often left out. Maltese say il-Belt.

Birżebbuġa: il-bir means well, iż-żebbuġa is one olive.

Bormla (or Cospicua): il-bir is the well, Mulej means Lord.

Fgura: il-figura means the figure, named after a statue.

Għarb: għarb means west, and it's a village on the west coast of Gozo.

Gżira: il-gżira means the island, after the Manoel island just near.

Iklin: il-klin means rosemary, after the many plants that were there before.

Marsa: il-marsa means harbor.

Marsaxlokk: il-marsa means harbor, ix-xlokk southeast. It is located in the southeast of Malta.

Mellieħa: il-melħ means salt in Maltese. There used to be saltpans to get salt out of the sea in ancient history.

Mellieħa

Msida: l-omm means mother, Sid means lord.

Munxar: il-munxar is a kind of saw.

Raħal Ġdid (or Paola): ir-raħal is a village, ġdid means new.

San Pawl il-Baħar (or Saint Paul's Bay): named after the shipwreck of Saint Paul. Il-baħar means the sea.

Sliema: is-sliema means safety.

Swieqi: is-swieq is the plural of is-suq, meaning market.

Żabbar: it-tiżbir is the pruning of trees, a way to grow trees better. Many specialists lived around the village.

Żebbuġ: iż-żebbuġ means olives, named after the many olive trees in the area.

Żejtun: iż-żejt means oil. Many oil producers live in Żejtun.

Bonus 2: study further on the internet

If you want to learn more Maltese, check out my other books, courses and extra resources via the links below:

Maltese online course: https://bit.ly/3WeVX3G

700+ everyday words and expressions:

100+ Maltese verbs explained:

More books to learn Maltese:
https://learn-any-language-with-alain.com/product-category/maltese/

More Maltese on: https://learn-any-language-with-alain.com/maltese/

The final word - About the author

We're at the end of the book - congratulations, you're much better prepared to learn Maltese.

About the author

Curiously, when Alain de Raymond was young, many language teachers told him he wasn't so good at languages. His Dutch was poor. His English teacher even advised him to follow extra courses.

He discovered he loved languages when he went to Germany in 2010. He had some basic German skills but started to speak in German from day one. What he got in return was amazing: friendship, love, respect and a good level of German. Since then, he's passionate about languages.

Now he's proud to be able to express himself in French, Dutch, English, German, Maltese and Spanish. He also has some Portuguese notions. And he's always busy learning new languages and taught some of his languages via tutoring.

He also has a life besides languages. He loves economics, politics and all the processes that shape society. He worked in communications a few years and holds 3 degrees: in Journalism, EU Studies and Management.

www.ingramcontent.com/pod-product-compliance
Ingram Content Group UK Ltd.
Pitfield, Milton Keynes, MK11 3LW, UK
UKHW041313220425
5564UKWH00035B/506